SCORPIONS!

A MY INCREDIBLE WORLD PICTURE BOOK

MY INCREDIBLE WORLD

Copyright © 2023, My Incredible World

All rights reserved. This book or any portion thereof may not be reproduced or used in any manner whatsoever without the express written permission of the copyright holder.

www.myincredibleworld.com

Scorpions are **arachnids**, which means they are related to spiders, ticks, and mites.

Scorpions are found on every continent except Antarctica.

They have been around for millions of years and are considered ancient creatures.

There are over 2,000 different species of scorpions around the world!

They can vary in size from as tiny as 2.5 mm up to more than 8 inches (20 cm) long!

Scorpions have a tough **exoskeleton** that protects their bodies.

They are known for their distinctive pincers or claws, called **pedipalps**, which they use to catch and hold prey.

Scorpions also have a long, curved tail with a **stinger** at the end.

They use their stingers to inject venom into their prey or to defend themselves.

Scorpions have organs on their belly called **pectines**, which help them detect vibrations in the ground!

They are primarily **nocturnal**, meaning they are most active at night.

Scorpions are strictly **carnivorous**, which means they only eat meat.

They are excellent hunters, capturing and eating insects, spiders, and even other scorpions!

Scorpions glow under ultraviolet light due to chemicals in their exoskeletons!

As they grow, they shed their exoskeletons in a process called **molting**.

Female scorpions give birth to live young, rather than laying eggs.

Baby scorpions, called **scorplings**, ride on their mother's back until they are old enough to survive on their own.

Scorpions have a unique way of walking called a **scuttle**, where they move sideways.

Their average lifespan ranges from about 2 to 10 years, depending on the species.

Scorpions can be found in a wide range of habitats, including deserts, rainforests, grasslands, and mountains!

They can survive in extreme conditions, and can even go without food for up to a year!

Scorpions are incredible!

Printed in Great Britain
by Amazon